Cutting-Edge STEM

Cutting-Edge Blockchain and Bitcoin

Kevin Kurtz

Lerner Publications ◆ Minneapolis

Lerner Publications Company
An imprint of Lerner Publishing Group, Inc.
241 First Avenue North
Minneapolis, MN 55401 USA

For reading levels and more information, look up this title
at www.lernerbooks.com.

Main body text set in Adrianna Regular 14/20.
Typeface provided by Chank.

Library of Congress Cataloging-in-Publication Data

Names: Kurtz, Kevin, author.
Title: Cutting-edge blockchain and bitcoin / Kevin Kurtz.
Description: Minneapolis, MN : Lerner Publishing Group, Inc., [2020] | Series: Searchlight books. Cutting-edge stem | Includes bibliographical references and index. | Audience: Age 8–11. | Audience: Grades 4 to 6.
Identifiers: LCCN 2019011151 (print) | LCCN 2019016646 (ebook) | ISBN 9781541583429 (eb pdf) | ISBN 9781541576803 (lb : alk. paper) | ISBN 9781541583429 (ebook)
Subjects: LCSH: Bitcoin—Juvenile literature. | Electronic funds transfers | Digital currency—Juvenile literature. | Cryptocurrencies—Juvenile literature.
Classification: LCC HG1710 (ebook) | LCC HG1710 .K875 2019 (print) | DDC 332.4—dc23

LC record available at https://lccn.loc.gov/2019011151

Manufactured in the United States of America
1-46662-47658-8/16/2019

Contents

Chapter 1

WHAT IS BITCOIN?

Kama has money in her smartphone. She can use it to buy things online, from sneakers to a brand-new car. But Kama can never touch this money. It exists only as computer code.

Imagine if coins or paper money no longer existed.

Bitcoin is not a real coin. But people often understand it better by imagining it is.

One day, Kama's digital money might be worth $4,000. Another day it might rise to $5,000 or drop down to $3,000. Its value changes all the time.

This digital money is bitcoin. People use it around the world. Bitcoin has even made some people rich.

Digital Money

A bitcoin is not actually a coin. A computer program creates bitcoins. They are information stored on people's digital devices.

Bitcoins appear as lines of code on a computer or other digital device.

BitPay is one example of a bitcoin
wallet app.

To use bitcoins, you need a bitcoin wallet app. You buy
bitcoins with regular money and store them in your wallet
app. Each bitcoin wallet has an online address. When you
buy something with bitcoins, you get the online address
of the seller's wallet. Your wallet uses the address to
transfer the bitcoins to the seller's wallet.

What Are Bitcoins Worth?

Bitcoins have value because people believe they do. That's the same reason any kind of money has value. A dollar bill is a piece of paper, but the paper itself is not actually worth one dollar. Instead, the paper bill is just a symbol of value. Because everyone believes a dollar bill is worth one dollar, people feel confident using it to buy and sell things.

HOW MUCH DO YOU THINK THIS PIECE OF PAPER IS REALLY WORTH?

Governments used to stash away large amounts of gold as a way to ensure the value of their money.

People have other reasons to trust the value of money. Big institutions such as governments also believe in its value. This allows the value of money to remain stable over a long period.

Hardly any governments believe in the value of bitcoins. Bitcoins' value depends on the law of supply and demand.

Supply and Demand

If there is more demand for something than the supply of it, the price of that thing goes up. Say you have ten bitcoins and not many people want to purchase one. If you sell them anyway, the price for each bitcoin will be low. But what if hundreds of people want to buy your ten bitcoins? Because the demand is much higher than the supply, the bitcoins can become really expensive. People will try to outbid one another to get one of your bitcoins.

Why don't governments print more money to become richer? The law of supply and demand leads to inflation. Inflation means that as governments print more money, that money becomes less valuable.

In 2017, ten thousand bitcoins could have bought over ten million pizzas!

A mysterious programmer first created bitcoins in 2009. Then, there was no demand for them, and they were worth less than one cent. One of the first people to use bitcoins spent ten thousand of them to buy two large pizzas.

Over time, more people became interested in bitcoins. As the demand increased, the value of bitcoins rose. In 2017, the demand exploded. Thousands of people wanted bitcoins. At one point that year, ten thousand bitcoins would have bought more than thirteen million large pizzas!

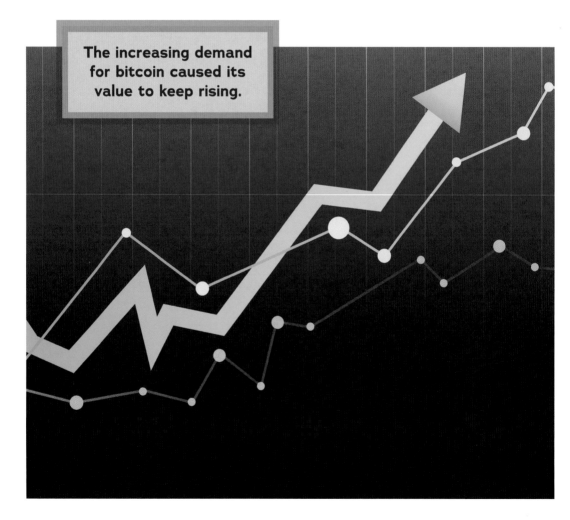

The increasing demand for bitcoin caused its value to keep rising.

No one knows who created bitcoin and blockchain.

That's a fact!

The programmer of bitcoin and blockchain used the made-up name Satoshi Nakamoto. Nakamoto's real identity is a mystery. Nakamoto could be a woman or a man. It could even be a group of people. Nakamoto communicated only online, and no one has heard from Nakamoto since 2011.

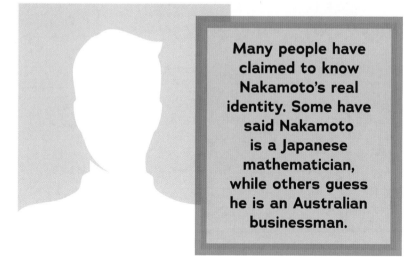

Many people have claimed to know Nakamoto's real identity. Some have said Nakamoto is a Japanese mathematician, while others guess he is an Australian businessman.

Chapter 2

WHAT IS BLOCKCHAIN?

Look at a ten- or twenty-dollar bill. You will see a variety of colors, shapes, and even shiny numbers. The symbols and numbers make paper bills hard to counterfeit, or copy. If it were easy to copy paper bills, people would stop trusting that they have value.

A police agent shows counterfeit US bills. How could you tell these bills are counterfeit?

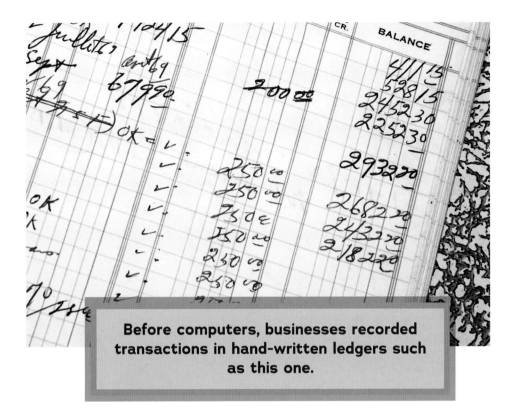

Before computers, businesses recorded transactions in hand-written ledgers such as this one.

Countering Counterfeiting

The idea of digital money has been around for a long time. But digital currency was easy to counterfeit, lowering its value. Since digital money is just computer code, anyone could use the code to make more money.

The creator of bitcoin solved this problem by inventing the blockchain. The blockchain is like a public ledger. Ledgers are notebooks or computer documents where businesses record their sales. Whenever a business receives or spends money, it records the transaction in a ledger.

Blockchain is a digital ledger. Anyone with bitcoins can see it. The blockchain shows each time a bitcoin passes from one bitcoin wallet to another. It keeps track of where a bitcoin is supposed to be. For example, if the blockchain shows a bitcoin is in wallet A, but wallet B is trying to spend it, then wallet B must be using a counterfeit. Blockchain allows everyone to be sure bitcoins are real.

The blockchain works because many people are reviewing its transactions at all times.

Bitcoin and Blockchain in Action

People called miners create the blockchain. They use computers to verify the latest bitcoin transactions, or make sure the transactions are correct. Then miners add a record of the transactions to the blockchain. But miners don't do this for fun. The first miner to verify the transactions gets the code for a blank bitcoin transaction, worth about 12.5 bitcoins. Because the transaction has no receiver listed, miners can send the 12.5 bitcoins to themselves. These bitcoins are the reward for building the blockchain.

Miners need a lot of hardware to check bitcoin transactions.

Chapter 3

BITCOIN TAKES OFF

At first, the value of bitcoins rose very slowly. It took two years for one bitcoin to be worth one dollar. As people realized the value of bitcoins could keep growing, a lot more people became interested in them. Over time, the demand for bitcoins grew.

Between 2009 and 2017, the worth of these bitcoins went from pennies to thousands of dollars.

As bitcoins' value rose, entrepreneurs such as Cameron and Tyler Winklevoss began to invest in digital currency.

Buy Bitcoin

The more people wanted bitcoin, the more its value went up. The media reported more and more stories about bitcoins. That helped the demand for them to rise even higher. By 2013, one bitcoin was worth hundreds of US dollars.

Then, in 2017, the demand for bitcoins soared. Thousands of people tried to buy them, and their value skyrocketed. At one point that year, one bitcoin was worth $19,783.21!

Bye, Bitcoin

But bitcoins' high value did not last long. Almost everyone buying bitcoins in 2017 was hoping to get rich. People bought bitcoins at a low price and sold them at a higher one. Eventually, more people were selling bitcoins than were buying them. The supply became much higher than the demand, and the price of bitcoins dropped rapidly. Just one year after its high point, the value of a bitcoin had dropped by almost $16,000.

Even when bitcoins' value crashed, many people held onto them, hoping the value would increase again.

Millions of bitcoins have been lost forever.

It's true!

Some people bought bitcoins when their value was low and then forgot about them. When bitcoins became worth a lot of money, these people went looking for their bitcoin wallets. Unfortunately, many of them had gotten rid of or lost access to the device that held the wallet. Since the bitcoins existed only as code in the wallets, the money was gone forever. Three to four million bitcoins might have been permanently lost so far.

One way bitcoin is similar to physical money is if you lose it, it's gone forever!

Chapter 4

WHAT'S NEXT FOR BITCOIN AND BLOCKCHAIN?

More people know about bitcoins than ever before. But bitcoins are still not widely accepted. One study found that in the US, fewer than six million people regularly use bitcoins. That means the vast majority of people use them occasionally or not at all.

People have many reasons for avoiding bitcoin. They may think it's too hard to understand or that its value is too uncertain.

THE ETHEREUM CRYPTOCURRENCY FEATURES A COIN CALLED AN ETHER.

Some experts are confident that some kind of digital money will eventually become popular. In 2019, Facebook announced it would create its own digital currency called Libra. Many other digital currency systems already exist, such as Ethereum and Ripple. Some even think a successful digital currency could eliminate the need for paper money.

Coding Spotlight

It could be possible to program digital money to do things paper money can't do. For example, people could program digital coins to buy only certain things. These programmed digital coins are called colored coins. Parents could give kids their allowances in colored coins. The parents could program the coins to buy only certain kinds of snacks. The coins might buy pretzels, but not candy.

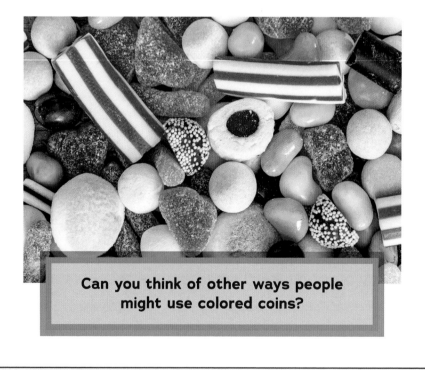

Can you think of other ways people might use colored coins?

Many new companies are already putting blockchain technology to use.

Blockchain Disrupts the Internet

Though bitcoin gets a lot of attention, blockchain might eventually have a bigger impact on people's lives. Blockchain allows individuals to connect directly with others on the internet.

Companies often use people's information to target them with advertisements or other services.

Big tech companies have huge data centers with thousands of computers called servers. Servers store and process the data of people who use the company's services. The companies charge people a fee for using their servers. Sometimes the fee is money the user must pay. Sometimes it is an indirect fee, such as collecting users' private information. Many people feel uneasy about how companies use their information.

That's where blockchain comes in. When people use blockchain, they don't need a company's services. Instead, blockchain uses a network of people's computers to store data. Blockchain users don't have to pay a fee or give out information.

Using blockchain, these two computers could connect directly instead of going through a server.

Many programmers are taking the idea of blockchain and using it in new ways. They are trying to create things like social networks and ride-sharing programs. A social network using blockchain could connect people directly to their friends without using a company such as Facebook. People using blockchain could keep complete control over their personal data.

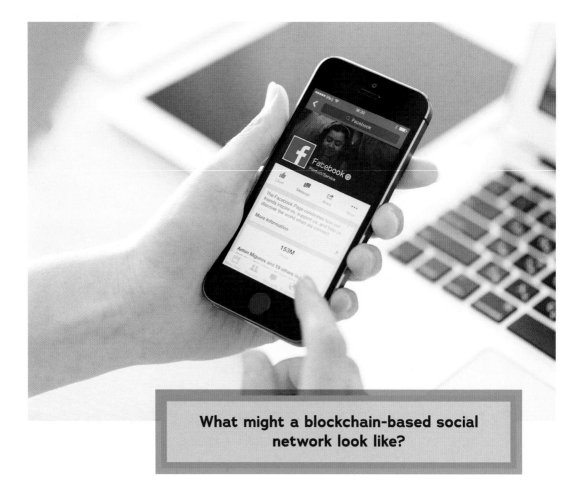

What might a blockchain-based social network look like?

People could use the blockchain instead of paying ride-sharing services to find drivers.

A ride-sharing blockchain program could directly find a nearby driver to pick you up. When you catch your ride, you would pay only your driver, not your driver and a ride-sharing company such as Uber.

The limits of bitcoin and blockchain technology are still unclear. But many users think they have a lot of potential. They could bring big changes to both money and the internet in the future.

Glossary

code: the written instructions that tell a computer program what to do

counterfeit: to make a copy of money illegally

currency: a system of money used by a country or a large group of people

demand: the number of people who want to buy something

ledger: a notebook or computer document used by businesses to record their sales

miner: any person who uses a computer to check bitcoin transactions and record them on blockchains in hopes of a reward of new bitcoins

supply: the number of items that are available to sell

transaction: the occurrence of buying or selling something

verify: to make sure something is correct

Learn More about Blockchain and Bitcoin

Books

Cribb, Joe. *Eyewitness Money.* New York: DK, 2016. This book shows what different kinds of money look like and how they are used.

Hollander, Barbara Gottfried. *Bitcoins: Navigating Open Source Currency.* New York: Rosen, 2015. Learn the basics of bitcoin, and dive into the history of this cryptocurrency

Lyons, Heather, and Elizabeth Tweedale. *Learn to Program.* Minneapolis: Lerner Publications, 2017. Read more about computer code and how to use it.

Websites

Blockchain for Kids
  https://lisk.io/academy/blockchain-basics/blockchain-for-kids
  A boy and his blue cat explain blockchain in this funny video.

Supply and Demand Facts for Kids
  https://kids.kiddle.co/Supply_and_demand
  Dig deeper into the law of supply and demand.

US Mint
  https://www.usmint.gov/learn/kids
  Learn how real coins work through games and activities.

Index

Photo Acknowledgments

Image credits: Westend61/Getty Images, p. 4; Parilov/Shutterstock.com, p. 5; oatawa/Shutterstock .com, p. 6; Piotr Swat/Shutterstock.com, p. 7; Andrey Lobachev/Shutterstock.com, p. 8;Timur Vildanov/Shutterstock.com, p. 9; skodonnell/E+/Getty Images, p. 10; New Africa/Shutterstock.com, p. 11; eightshot studio/Shutterstock.com, p. 12; Wiktoria Matynia/Shutterstock.com, p. 13; STR/AFP/ Getty Images, p. 14; FLariviere/Shutterstock.com, p. 15;G-Stock Studio/Shutterstock.com, p. 16; JUSTIN TALLIS/AFP/Getty Images, pp. 17, 22 Chesnot/Getty Images, pp. 18, 20; Astrid Stawiarz/ Getty Images, p. 19; George Frey/Getty Images, p. 21; Jack Taylor/Getty Images, p. 23; Tatyana Vyc/Shutterstock.com, p. 24; LuckyStep/Shutterstock.com, p. 25; Tetra images RF/Getty Images, p. 26; Pattanaphong Khuankaew/EyeEm/Getty Images, p. 27; Bloomicon/Shutterstock.com, p. 28; Nisian Hughes/The Image Bank/Getty Images, p. 29.

Cover: MARK GARLICK/SCIENCE PHOTO LIBRARY/Getty Images.